Whole Brain Theory
in Education

Whole Brain Theory in Education

Joyce Diane Schulz

Argosy University Inland Empire

Masters Research Thesis
Submitted to
School of Education
Argosy University
December, 2010

AuthorHouse™
1663 Liberty Drive
Bloomington, IN 47403
www.authorhouse.com
Phone: 1-800-839-8640

First published by AuthorHouse   05/20/2011

ISBN: 978-1-4567-6071-7 (sc)
ISBN: 978-1-4567-6072-4 (ebk)

Library of Congress Control Number: 2011908550

Printed in the United States of America

CONTENTS

TABLES (Figures)

ACKNOWLEDGEMENTS

The author of this thesis wishes to thank several professors for their patience and time at Argosy University Inland Empire. The first and foremost is Dr. Teresa Feller, a dedicated professor of Masters and Ph.d. thesis production. Her discipline editing helped the author realize how a Master's thesis paper was arranged and design. Without her constant, patient editing, this paper would not have been created. My other mentor has been Dr. Narcisa Skeete, with her years of educational experience gave me humor and laughter with the difficult process of Graduate Studies. Also to my friend Judy Rangel, a retired ESL, Spanish teacher, who helped me gain understanding about second language acquisition students and how they have unique learning styles. The biggest help was my friend and student Kali Pratim Chourduray from Bangdelesh India, who helped me over come my emotional distress by giving me positive motivation to continue my quest.

ABSTRACT

The purpose of this study is to examine the need for learners to identify their dominant learning modality, as understood by the eight Multiple intelligences of Howard Gardner (Gardner,1993), the intelligences of right/left brain dominance-processing fields (Herrman, 1995; Jensen, 1998; Katzir, 2003) and some of the researchers in the whole brain theory. This is part of the Whole Brain learning theory, which is also called the Balanced Whole learner, Whole Mind/Open mind learning methods. The right/left brain processing seems to be part of the multiple intelligence preference fields (Connell, 1996). Fifty secondary students, ten diverse adult learners, two administrators, and eight teachers were part of the surveys done through 2009-2010.

The questions that were asking whether or nor the adult learners or students were aware of the learning style preferences, and did they want to know them? The second focus was did their heritage, language, culture, educational level, or gender affect their learning style preferences. The researcher found positive data that supports these issues. The other information supports that brain dominance, MI intelligence theories are interwoven within each other as a composite Whole Brain Learning Theory. The study gives resources, findings and recommendations on how it can be implemented in a public school learning environment. The modalities can be integrated in a composite whole, and not separate categories, but an interwoven process to discover a person's brain processing. This can be a process for an administrator, teacher, student, and adults to understand their unique method of processing information called the Whole Brain Learning Theory of Education.

PERSONAL PHILOSOPHY OF EDUCATION

By

Joyce Diane Schulz

Argosy University Online

After spending close to thirty years in the California Public school sector, as a contractual teacher, long-term substitute, independent study teacher, and daily substitute; I developed a perspective on the public schools in general. I have worked all over California, in rural, urban, and farm areas. Each learning environment was a reflection of the community it served. It was when I worked in a Montessori learning environment and alternative education that I began to have some glimpses of what learning was about. I also worked in child development centers, which ran on a learning modalities curriculum, with sensory training, and concrete applications. I had not really tried to break apart all the components of the learning process until I went back to graduate school.

Education for me is the doctrine of the life long learner. To the moment we are born, and to our death, we are in the process of learning some new information, or feeding the database in our brain. Education is not being fed facts like a database, but a reflective process, which makes positive citizens in the global area of shared values and ethics. It is the vehicle to give us skills and abilities to survive in this pluralistic society. We are part of a pluralistic society, and how we relate to our global family will make or break our survival. We are not isolated beings, but part of a global community, which feeds our positive contributions to the world. Education shapes our visions, and it comes from those who came before us, ancient, present, and future. Education informs us where we need to go and how we can share our vision with others. Without the educational process, we might as well go the way of tribal technology. Education is the doctrine to help us survive in this technological, complex world systems.

Each district where I have taught, has had diverse learners. My question was why certain children, when taught the same material did not process the information well. Some students were labeled slow or lazy. Then I realized even in the middle school and secondary level, the problems still seem to exist. Students were then tested for special education, etc, and there were all kinds of rationale explaining why certain students just did not learn or "get it"

While working in pre-schools and public schools at all levels, I came across the Howard Gardner's Multiple Intelligences in the 90's. It seem to make sense to me. I was director of a small private elementary school in the Big Bear Mountains and we began some experimentation in learning techniques with MI intelligences. I began to be a strong believer in the individualized center at the primary level, and a diverse group system for the intermediate level, the middle school, with the secondary level a mixed brain theory level. It is the curriculum of the national, state, and local districts that has the power to help every student learn.

With over crowded classrooms and rigid instructional guidelines, teachers had no choice but to teach in a secondary setting to all students regardless of their learning problems. It is called the Learning for Mastery model or LPM (Ornstein, 2008). This did not serve the individual student very well, and some low level federal programs have been instituted in the high school, which helps these struggling students. I had worked in these classes, and the students were glad to have these lower level classes, which did not cause them stress of achievement. These low-level students, behaved like right brain, kinesthetic, visual/spatial, interpersonal, computer based learners.

From the perspective of the teacher, she/he is a role model, and a clarified guide to help direct the individual learner to understand what the knowledge based lesson is all about. When you have a group of low-level learners who function differently than the rest of the left-brain motivated learners, they need special attention or they "turn off" to the information being addressed. They have learned how not to learn, and barely make it through their school experiences. After discovering the neuroscience of learning and brain activity, I concluded that MI intelligence, and cultural impact on student's learning potential; I decided to become a mentor or specialist in Whole Brain Theory.

I am a supporter of long distance education with video and satellite systems, and know that technology can help all learners to learn, to access information and observe viewpoints from around the world globally. This is a target for the multiculturism that everyone needs to be expose to. Our cultural backgrounds are necessary components for knowledge about ourselves, and our ancestor backgrounds (Banks, 2006). Students need to observe the differences in cultures, and how it relates to their lives. It helps to create the lifelong learning belief that I advocate. We are forced to reinvent ourselves through our lives, because of the rapid social, technological, and economic change, which have occurred globally (Ornstein, 2006).

The National curriculum standards have changed and have funded the development of national curriculum standards in seven subject fields: history, geography, economics, English, foreign Languages, mathematics and science. It is the back to basics proponents to try to restore the primacy of basic content to the curriculum, and the federal government, which offers financial incentives for states to adopt the national curriculum standards, regardless of the community needs of a particular district (Ornstein, 2006 pg. 439). Again this is a top down approach to learning and organization, which does not solve the individual or student-centered needs.

Curriculum and learning theories should evolve to serve a changing society. New knowledge, indeed, is not necessarily better than old knowledge. We need to cut away old and irrelevant parts of the curriculum and to integrate and balance new knowledge. As we modify and update content, we need to protect schools and students against fads and frills, and extreme points of view. We must keep in perspective the type of society we have, the values we cherish, and the educational goals we wish to achieve (Ornstein, 2006, pg. 442). Whole Brain learning is commonly thought that the left and right hemispheres of the brain have different functions; the left hemisphere is used for analytical operations, written and spoken language and logical processes. The right hemisphere is involved with visualizations, synthesis, and creativity. Some people have skills that indicate that they operate in one hemisphere more than the other. Although more recent brain imaging techniques have shown that the notion of a differentiation of brain functions into left and right halves may be far too simplistic; it is clear that formal education system have tended to emphasis a rather narrow range of brain capabilities, which the standardized testing procedure use.

Whole brain learning uses techniques that integrate the synthetic and imaginative brain skills with the analytical and language skills. Simple strategies such an MI curriculum and instructional activities, can make better use of the whole brain and can dramatically improve learning and performance skills (Shearer, 2006) Then with the use of computers as tools for research, Internet browsing, and multimedia skills, especially the implementation of the web design, with power point presentations, Microsoft lessons, the student can have an whole brain experience, rather going through a static text book experience.

Along with the individual student-centered learning, diagnostic items for assessment are needed in the in the cooperative learning process. This is part of the multicultural learning experiences. Students work with each other to accomplish a shared or common goal. The goal is reached through interdependence among all the group members rather than working alone. Each member is responsible for the outcome of the shared goal. Cooperative learning can produce greater student achievement than traditional learning methodologies. Students who work individually often compete against others to gain praise or other forms of rewards and reinforcements. The success of these individual

for the success of an achievement (Gibbs, 1994)

This idea of cooperative learning is to change the traditional structure by reducing competition and increasing cooperation among students, thus diminishing possible hostility and tension among students and raising the academic achievement of all (Ornstein, 2008 pg 430) It also reinforces team work, and cultures working together for a common goal thru cooperation.

Part of the naturalist intelligence of MI comes the knowledge of whole systems. It involves thinking in several shifts form mechanistic, reductionistic thinking. It is the shift from the parts to the whole, which is again a right brain function. According to the systems view a living system has essential properties which none of the parts have. They arise from the interaction and relationships between the parts. These properties are destroyed when the system is dissected, either physically or theoretically, into isolated elements. This is a form of whole brain thinking and learning. There is more information, which is part of my capstone (Capra, 1995).

Also in my philosophy is the understanding a student's emotional literacy. Certain diagnostic tests are available to help students recognize how they function emotionally under stressful conditions. It is all part of the MI theory of Meta cognition. There are resources of the meditation practice that promotes a change of a relax alpha waves of biofeedback, which is helpful to produce a better learning atmosphere for the student.

One thing I have recognized that we cannot accommodate all learners with individual lesson plans in the public school system, but knowing how your students learn and behave internally, in a group or by themselves, will create a more positive teaching and learning atmosphere. The top down system of curriculum functions will be more effective, if there is a bottom up interaction as well.

Always from ancient times, it was the elite who received education as one of the methods of authority. We do try in the public democratic system to provide everyone with an education, but it is up to the individual to use it for his or her own good, and take advantage of it. In the poorer countries of the world, to be able to read and write is a rare Treasure. Here in America, education for our youth is slowly dissipating. Education should be our prime agenda for our nation, and presently the future is a foggy issue.

Joyce Diane Schulz
2011

REFERENCES

Banks, J.A (2006) Cultural Diversity and Education, Foundations, Curriculum and Teaching. Boston, MA: Pearson Education Inc.

Capra, F. (1995) From the Parts to the Whole, in the Education Network. Sydney Australian: Australian Education Network.

Gibbs, J. (1994) Tribes-A New Way of Learning Together. Windsor, CA: Centre Source Publications.

Lazcar D. (1990) Seven Ways of Knowing. Boston MA: Hawker Blownlow Education.

Ornstein, A.C. & Levine, D.U. Foundations of Education, Boston MA: Houghton Mifflin.

Shearer, C.B. (2006) Using a Multiple Intelligences Assessment to Facilitate Teacher Development: Kent University.

Wiggins, G. & McTighe, J. (2005). Understanding by Design. Upper Saddle River, NJ: Pearson Merrill Prentice Hall.

CHAPTER ONE

INTRODUCTION

At the turn of this century, our global world is connected by a series of webs of technological, visual/spatial/auditory images, and patterns. We, with our children, are bombarded with auditory/visual explosions of information. Thus, we live in a complex, stimulated, visual world not known a century ago. Students come to school with an exposure to visual/spatial/auditory images from the television, home computers, game boys, video games, and other technological devices to stimulate our multiple, sensory field (Brackin, 2000). These devices, unless interactive, do not really engage all students in the educational process. So the young child from birth is given a strong visual/spatial/auditory preference in his/her everyday life. Outer technological devices become exciting learning toys for entertainment. Thus, these toys become a normal method to acquire information.

Everywhere we look in our urban society, we are confronted with visual readouts, and displays which give us the information needed to function within it. This entertaining outer stimulus, is part of a positive, exciting world of lively, happy experiences. "It is no longer uncommon to see pictures being taken and sent from one mobile phone to another" (Brackin, 2000 pp.1). This technology gives us an access to visual-auditory and other forms of information, never before seen in anytime in history. This means that our students, and adults are more exposed to the visual/auditory learning process than ever before. It also means that they are somewhat desensitized to the visual stimulations, unless auditory stimulus is part of it. They may expect school to be part of the entertainment process, and learning is a fun process.

Students are made to fit into a learning system, which is generally rigid, systematized curriculum. It does not focus on the whole learner. If the different learner can not fit in this conformist framework, the individual falls into a maze of negative school experiences (Silverman, 1986).

Background of the Study

The term Whole Brain Learning may have to be redefined in the context of the learning acquisition. Intelligences may be more a physical action of the brain, while brain dominance is the inner processing of the brain, an integration of the visual perceptual field, or memory and imagery functions. Auditory is how we hear sounds, with the brain processing the vibration. Susan Ackerman writes about James L. Watson's concept (1992) from the article "Discovering the Brain," "Despite the fact that both the left and right hemispheres of your brain work together, they are not exactly the same. Each side differs from the other slightly in its functions and processes" (Ackerman, 1992).

1

The dominance of the left-brain activity, response to sight, hearing, taste, touch, and smell through words is superficial, and analytical. The right half of the brain helps you feel the whole of what you perceive. This is important because it indicates that all learners or both brain types are able to process visual information, but it is through the auditory/spatial process that it becomes a differentiation characteristic (Brackin, 2000 pp.2).

Especially in the cognitive process this concept becomes clearer. It is important to understand both parts of the Whole Brain needs to work in unison with all the modalities to have a balanced learner. Our world is becoming more visual/spatial/auditory overload. This may cause many distractive, disorders in many learners of all ages. They choose what modality they are comfortable with, from conditioning, which comes from outside of the home primarily. How they choose to use this input, or learning activities will be explored in this study. Regardless of the school situation, the researcher feels everyone should havesome idea how they learn neurologically, and conceptually for better communication in the teaching or the business field (Herrmann, 1995).

Purpose of the Study

The purpose of this study is to identify what the Whole Brain learning is about, within the context of Brain dominance and the Multiple Intelligences. It is supportive for a learner to discover all their dominant modalities and the right/left hemispheric orientations, which they function from. Brain dominance is part of the Whole Brain theory, and so is MI intellences. According to Garrietson (1979), activities in external seeing, and hearing are indicators of early visual, phonetic learning? Along with visual aspect, spatial reasoning is also operational with students of all ages. These diverse ways of relating to the world have powerful evolutionary changes throughout history in the development of various philosophies, religions, cultures, branches of sciences, and psychological theories (Silverman, 1986).

Statement of the Problem

With our society becoming more technologically focused, our future educators need to understand the importance of Whole Brain processing. Whole brain leaning uses methods that integrate the synthetic and imaginative brain skills with analytical and language skills. Simple methods can improve learning and performance skills (Caine, 1999). There are some important guidelines that needs to be understood in the Whole Brain educational field.

- Brain is a parallel process—it is always doing multiple tasks.
- Learning involves the complete body and mind, and both parts influence this process.
- Meaning is a constant operation, channel and focused.
- The brain is designed to perceive and generate patterns, and resists meaningless information upon it.
- Emotions are critical to the learning process and can affect the learning process.
- The brain processes the whole with the parts conceptually, so both hemispheres are inter-connective.
- Information is stored in multiple areas of the brain, and can be retrieved through multiple memories and neutral pathways.
- Humans search for meaning is innate.
- Meaning is more important than just informational facts.

- We have two types of memory: spatial and rote.
- We comprehend better when facts are embedded in our natural spatial memory.
- The brain is social and develops better in inter relationships with others.
- Learning is developmental.
- Learning involves conscious and unconscious processes. We learn more than we perceived consciously.
- Our Brains have different ways of organizing memory.
- Learning involves both focused attention and peripheral perception.
- Learning occurs best in an atmosphere that is low in threat and high in challenges.
- Each brain is unique, and not all people learn the same (Caine, 1999; Tramo, 1995).

Research Questions

The following research questions will the basis for the review of Literature and focus of the study

1. Are students and adults aware of their own learning style preferences?
2. Do the participant's heritage, language, culture, educational level, or gender affect the participants learning style preferences?

Significance of the Study

This study can be significant to the educational community in numerous ways. Educators can use this study to evaluate the student's learning dominance in the Whole Brain Theory, which guide teachers to balance students' intelligences within the learning activity. The use of multimedia, computers, and manipulative supplements the modalities completely. Recognizing the specific brain intelligence and modalities can help the learner have better communication in the learning environment. This study becomes a holistic approach to learning within a multi-faceted and flexible definition of the MI intelligences, and brain dominances, which includes all types of knowledge (Jensen, 1998).

Assumptions

A series of inventory surveys have been given to a select group of high school students, teachers, and diverse adult learners. They are from diverse, cultural backgrounds. The participant's answers comprised the researcher's data and analysis findings. Survey responses were assumed to have been answered honestly, based on the individual experiences of each participant. It was assumed that high school secondary students would be more homogenous in their preferences than the diverse group of adult learners. It was assumed that language and culture might affect the preferences of the adult learners due to their maturity.

Limitations

Limitations are factors outside of the researcher's control. The number of secondary teachers available for the survey questions is a limitation, due to the teachers' professional time constraints. The researcher was denied access to colleges and high schools, as she is retired and not a current member of the district. This limited the choice of participants to the researcher's own community. An attempt was made to send out surveys online, but the response rate was not sufficient for an adequate research sample.

Delimitations

Delimitations are factors that the researcher controls. Delimitations to this study are as follows: First the researcher chose to do this study with high school students, teachers, and adult learners. Also, the surveys or inventories needed to come back so they could be evaluated by the test database for evaluation. The researcher searched for the participants from the schools, community centers, and diverse populations in her area. The researcher because of copyrights, create the surveys from several other internet sources, which fitted the adult learner characteristics.

Definitions

Technology
Technology is the knowledge or application of knowledge, which comes from the industrial, applied scientific arts. It is the properties of materials and concepts of certain functions, processes, and phenomena; which can provide solutions to environmental, or technical problems. (Gaxiola, 2003)

Computer
A mechanical device used for computing, which by means of stored instructions, and information, performs rapid, often complex, calculations or complies, correlates, and selects data (Webster's, 1975).

Multiple Intelligences
Howard Gardner, a Harvard Psychologist, developed a theory of intelligence, which falls into a least nine separate modalities. They are: Linguistic or verbal, musical, logical-mathematical, bodily kinesthetic, interpersonal or understanding of others, intrapersonal or understanding of self, spatial/visual, naturalist, and metaphysical intelligence (Gardner, 1993).

Visual/Spatial Modality (VSL)
The visual-spatial learner (VSL) model is based on the new discoveries in brain research about the different functions of the hemispheres. The visual-spatial learners are individuals who think in pictures rather in words. They need to learn visually than auditorally. They learn all at once, and generally have good memories. They do not learn easily in a sequential manner, but are able to make solutions without showing their work. They are systems thinkers who can manage large amounts of information from different directions. They are not detailed orientate (Silverman, 1986).

Right and Left Brain hemispheres
This concept is one of the new discoveries in brain research about the different functions of the hemispheres. This theory has been in neurosciences for some time. It is just accepted in the Whole Brain theory, but sometimes it is to simple to have credibility. The left hemisphere is sequential, analytical, and time-oriented. The right hemisphere perceives the whole, synthesizes, and apprehends movement in space (Silverman, 1986). There is also the whole brain functioning, which is the goal for optimal learning,so the student can assess both brain hemispheres equally. This is your balanced learner and the goal of the Whole Brain learning theory (Power, 1997; Lundsten, 1997).

Whole Brain Theory

Brain-based learning is a multi faceted approach to instruction using current research from Neuroscience. Whole brain theory is education focused on how the brain learns naturally and is based on the actual structure and function of the human brain at varying developmental states.

From the research is a biologically drive framework for creating effective instruction. This theory helps explain recurring learning behaviors, and is a meta-concept that includes a diverse mix of techniques. It can include such educational concepts like:

1. Mastery learning,
2. Experimental learning,
3. Learning styles,
4. Multiple Intelligences,
5. Cooperative learning,
6. Practical simulations,
7. Problem based learning
8. Movement education (Joyce, B., Well. M., Calhoun E., 2009)

Whole Brain Theory

Brain-based learning is a multi faceted approach to instruction using current research from Neuroscience. Whole brain theory is education focused on how the brain learns naturally and is based on the actual structure and function of the human brain at varying developmental states.

From the research is a biologically driven framework for creating effective instruction.

This theory helps explain recurring learning behaviors, and is meta-concept that includes a diverse mix of techniques. It can include such education concepts like:

1. Mastery learning.
2. Experimental learning.
3. Learning styles.
4. Multiple Intelligences
5. Cooperative learning.
6. Practical simulations.
7. Problem based learning.
8. Movement education (Calhoun E., 2009; Joyce, B 2009.; Hoerr, 2000).

Summary

Due to the fact that our increasing society is becoming more visual/spatial/auditory with the advance of technology, our classroom teachers need to be more aware of the Whole Brain Theory and how it may have implications for secondary and adult learners. Since our society constantly experiences exposure to computers and multi-media marketing which stimulates the brain, secondary students have become accustomed to this type of preference and may react more positively

or three-dimensional objects to solve a question. The Whole Brain Theory gives the educators a guideline of valid neuro-scientific research, which can inform the teacher how students learn at different stages of development.

Through the use of surveys, tests, and observations, the data obtained from this research May help to identify dominant intelligences and processing for the learner. This brain processing information may help students work on various exercises to balance their less dominant intelligences, thus increase their learning potentiality. Preference surveys may help educators know how the individual learner's style might be positively affected while learning a particular subject.

Chapter Two will provide a review of the literature focused on the Whole Brain Theory in the various learning activities and their validity in the learning environment.

CHAPTER TWO

REVIEW OF THE LITERATURE

The purpose of this chapter is to present a review of the literature focused on major themes of the multiple intelligence learners, whole brain theories, and brain dominances. Many teachers have a problem with the time management of teaching the Whole Brain applications. They are not trained to recognize these learning styles. They also have little knowledge of the right brain verses left brain-learning activities. Without having some background experiences in the field of Multiple Intelligences applications, it can be a foreign world to many teachers, young or seasoned. Yet more adult students are choosing the MI intelligences way of learning with various academic skills. Students generally function in more than one modality, and the balanced learning uses most of the several modalities in unison (Silverman, 1986).

One example can be that there are two kinds of seeing: the external seeing, and the spatial observation. It is the brain's ability to interpret "external seeing," which is complex and multi-faceted. Through the two processes of "visual contrasting images" and "pattern seeking" the learner acquires information visually. This is part of the spatial reality of the right brain function, which spatial connections. One makes conceptual creations in the imagination, which is the imagery process or mind pictures called visualizations. The flexibility of the mind to make connections helps learners break away from objectivity and enter a realm of imaginative reality, which can lies within an object or idea. The process of drawing objects realistically, patterning with color images, and building three dimensional block structures, is an external seeing process. When it takes a critical process for balance, it becomes a spatial modality. This is an internal process of observation, which is sometimes felt, but not seen. It is clear that perception, or how we know what we know, is closely related (Brackin, 2000). If our knowledge is limited or not complete, then our perceptions of a visual reality becomes disorganized as well. With all this visually based technology around us, and accepted as part of our lives, the question arises of whether or not certain people who have a disadvantage because they are not visually oriented, are hindered by the shift towards the visual media (Garritson, 1979). This means certain people are developed with a dominant visual/spatial preference in cognitive, learning processes. The conclusion is that despite the lack of visual input, those with visual weakness do believe that such comparisons are virtually impossible to detect because finding comparable tests are so difficult (Hallahan, 2000).

This is one example where a student with p   a right brain function, or sequential aspects is learning mathematics, one of the following may occur, the student may:

(a) Be confused when learning multi-step procedures.
(b) Have trouble ordering the steps used to solve a problem.
(c) Feel overloaded when faced with a worksheet full of math exercises.
(d) Not be able to copy problems correctly.
(e) May have difficulties reading the hands on an analog clock.
(f) May have difficulties interpreting and manipulating geometric configurations.
(g) May have difficulties appreciating changes in objects as they are moved in space (Lauren, 2008).

Criticisms of the Use of Multiple Intelligences in the Classroom

The theory of the Multiple Intelligence learning theory, created by Howard Gardner, was a revolutionary idea in 1965. In its simplest form, Gardner proposed that intelligence, and all learning falls into at least nine separate modalities. Most of his research was done with the gifted and talented students in the area of creativity research (Maker, 1995). Another area of research was done with persons who have abnormal brains due to accident, disease, or stroke (Gardner, 1974). A holistic whole brain approach to MI's might emphasize the dynamic interplay of all intelligences, both within self and collaboratively with others, through a meta-cognitive process

The Nine Modalities or Intelligences are:

- **Linguistic or verbal**,—learns through words, written and spoken
- **Musical**,-deals with rhythmic and tonal patterns
- **Logical-mathematical**,—deals with numbers, symbols and abstract patterns.
- **Bodily-kinesthetic**,—deals with body and movement.
- **Interpersonal** (understanding of others),—deals with verbal and non-verbal communication with others.
- **Intrapersonal** (understanding of self)—deals with internal aspects of the self, and spiritual realities.
- **Spatial or visual**,—Deals in images and pictures, can visualize, create design and communicate with diagrams.
- **Naturalist**—learns through patterns in the natural environment, recognition and classification of objects in the natural environment.
- **Existential**—Learns through deep reflective questioning and meditation.

Below is a table illustration of the dissection of the brain, and the areas of intelligence, by Robert Sperry, noble peace prize 1981 winner. You will notice how the MI intelligences fit with the right and left brain Bi-sections (Sperry, 1969). This experimental work was done in the early 70's, and one would think Gardner might have seen this data of Sperry's.

Table 2.1

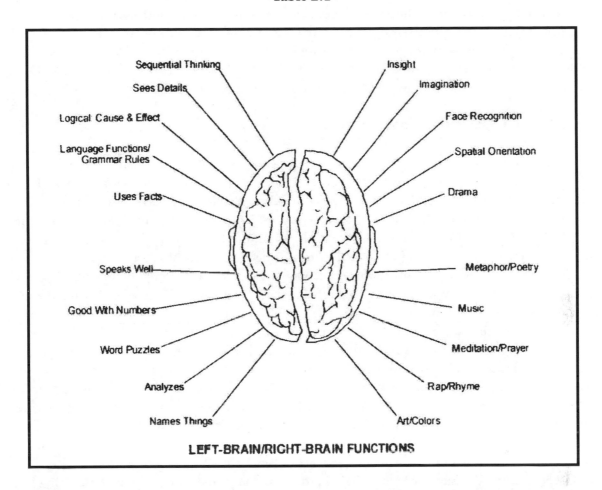

Sequential Thinking
Sees Details
Logical Cause & Effect
Language Functions/ Grammar Rules
Uses Facts
Speaks Well
Good With Numbers
Word Puzzles
Analyzes
Names Things

Insight
Imagination
Face Recognition
Spatial Orientation
Drama
Metaphor/Poetry
Music
Meditation/Prayer
Rap/Rhyme
Art/Colors

LEFT-BRAIN/RIGHT-BRAIN FUNCTIONS

The educational system today is not designed for these differences in learning. Many classrooms are not equipped with the simplest of technological equipment, especially in the primary classrooms. Time management remains to be a problem for the classroom teacher. Most of Gardner's ideas are based more on reasoning and intuition than on the results of the empirical research studies (Aiken, 1997). Also the nine intelligences are not of equal importance and value. Cultural differences do change varying levels of importance to the type of intelligence, regardless what Howard Gardner's research says (Banks, 2006).

Robert Steinberg (1985) asks whether an adult who is tone deaf and has no sense of rhythm can be considered mentally limited in the same way as one who has never developed any verbal skills. In 1938, Thurstone identified several primary mental abilities (verbal comprehension, numerical ability, spatial relations, perceptual speed, work fluency, memory and reasoning) that underlie all intellectual activities. According to Morgan (1996), identifying these various abilities and developing a theory that supports the many factors on intelligence has been a contribution to the area of study. Morgan believes that Gardner's nine intelligences might be better referred to as "cognitive styles" rather than constructs of intelligence (Morgan, 1996). Sternberg claims, "multiple intelligences might be referred

Many researchers feel that Gardner's MI is not legitimate because there are not qualitative specific tests to measure the nine intelligences. Gardner says a singularly psychometric approach to measuring intelligence based on paper and pencil tests is too limiting. Psychometrics is the psychological theory of mental measurement. Gardner recommends that any intelligence be assessed by a number of complementary approaches, which are the several core components of intelligence. For example, spatial intelligence might be assess by asking people to find their way around an unfamiliar terrain, to solve a abstract jigsaw puzzle, or to construct a three-dimension model of their home (Gardner, 1983). The scientific work C. Branton Shearer, Ph.d has done quantitive research work in MIDAS, a research foundation focus on MI validation (Shearer, 2006).

MI and the Classroom Environment

In the field of curriculum development, the implementation in the classroom is a mixed challenge. It is compelling for the instructor to finally expand his/her methods, techniques and strategies of teaching and go beyond the day-to-day, typical linguistic and logical tools commonly known as lecturing. Instructors filled the heads of the so-called empty minds with information, which becomes overfilled. This is called the traditional approach to learning. MI theory works to break this narrow and confined method of learning and remedy the one sidedness to teaching (Frey, 2008).

In the classroom environment, nowhere else, but in schools are large groups of individuals packed so closely together for so many hours, yet expected to perform at peak efficiency on difficult learning tasks and to interact harmoniously (Weinstein, 1979). MI theory indicates that the classroom environments require changes to aid the learning needs of the students.

In accepting the theory of Multiple Intelligences, teachers abandon traditional perspectives on intelligences. These new beliefs about intelligences influence the operation of schools within society. The operation of schools within societies provides a window on how those societies think about the realm of the intellect (Gardner, 1995). As teachers begin to implement new concepts of intelligence, they find themselves in a transitional phase in the classroom. Their beliefs are changing, and these concepts are reflected in their practice. Rosenthal and Jacobsen's studies conclude that teachers' beliefs significantly affect student performance (Rosenthal & Jacobsen, 1968).

Gardner does advocate a whole school approach to the introduction of an MI teaching and learning environment in a school. Education is individually configured for each student. The shaping of a whole school approach to the introduction of MI can be very gradual (Hyland, 2000). Hyland maintains that the easy introduction of MI in second level schools is inhibited by several factors, such as the prevailing view of intelligence, the influence of examinations, rigid subject boundaries and short class periods (Hyland, 2000). Others agree with McNiff, Fleischmann & Fitz Gibbon, 2000, that many external factors such as lack of planning time, dominance to traditional examinations, timetabling restrictions and lack of whole school support can have a negative impact on the introduction of MI into secondary schools (McNiff, Fleischmann, Fitz Gibbon, 2000)

However, advocates of MI theory have proposed many approaches for introducing MI practice in a school. Armstrong, demonstrates how a MI practice can take place informally in a traditional style class, where the teacher can lecture with rhythmic emphasis (musical), draws pictures on the board to illustrate points (spatial), makes dramatic gestures as she talks (bodily-kinesthetic), pauses to give students time to reflect (interpersonal), asks questions that invite spirited interaction (interpersonal), and includes references to nature in her lectures (naturalist).

While there is no prescriptive methods to teach among MI practitioners, there is agreement among them with regard to suitable strategies and techniques. Lazear, (1991), Bellanca (1998), Armstrong (2000), and Dickinson (2000) believe that any subject content can be taught with any of the intelligences and they can still use the same practical techniques, methods, tools and media for accessing the eight intelligences. Lazear, (1991) distinguishes between different lesson types by describing them as teaching for intelligence, teaching with an intelligence and teaching about an intelligence. Armstrong (2000) differentiates between teaching to an intelligence, and teaching through an intelligence. On the other hand, Bellancea (1998) does not make any distinctions between different MI lesson types. His examples rely heavily on visual/spatial and interpersonal activities to teach with/through and intelligence. Lazear's (1991) approach shows a concern with the process of learning and incorporates four stages of using an intelligence in his three lesson types. MI theory also points to the need to cater to individuality. Gardner believes that individually configured education may be more relevant to today's student than uniform schooling in which each student is expected to learn the same material in the same way.

The Right brain, and the Left-brain Functions

Many teachers try their best to accommodate the various learning styles of their students, but it is an over whelming task. There are a limited number of hours in the day, and even the most dedicated classroom teacher cannot plan for all the different learning styles and intelligences of his/her students. There are few research models available for solutions to the problems. Research has shown us that the right/left brain dominance preference inventories, is at the root of the MI preference scales, as well as part of the Whole Brain Learning Theory. They seem to have inter-connectiveness to each other.

The right brain, left brain model is based on the newest discoveries in brain research, focused mainly of the different functions of the hemispheres. It is directly related to the Multiple Intelligences theory. The left hemisphere is sequential, analytical, and time-oriented. The right hemisphere perceives the whole, and synthesizes, and apprehends movement in space. We need to balance both hemispheres as a harmony of the two functions engaged in a moving dance of inner balance of cognitive awareness. Most teachers have had little experience with their own brain orientation and dominant intelligence.

The concept of right brain and left-brain thinking developed form the research in the late 1960's of an American psycho-biologist Roger W. Sperry. See diagram 2.1. He discovered that the brain has two very different ways of thinking. Sperry was awarded a Nobel Prize in 1981, although subsequent research has showed brain processes are not as polarized or that simple. By better understanding our own neurological strengths and weaknesses, we can adapt our lessons to reach all of our students (Connell, 2009).

Whole Brain Theory

In 1976, while researching the brain as the source of creativity, Ned Herrmann learned of the pioneering brain research of Roger Sperry, Paul MacLean, Joseph Bogen and Michael Gazzanaga. From their work it is clear that the brain has four distinct and specialized structures. Inspired by this research, Herrmann worked with EEG scans and later, paper and pencil questionnaires to identify four distinct types of thinking, each roughly corresponding to one of the brain structures. The result of this Research is the Herrmann Whole Brain Model.

Teachers need to know what neurological style influences the way they teach. By understanding the process at work in the brain, we can better help our students explore their own individual

dominate. Teachers tend to communicate better with students who share their same neurological strengths. For example, a strong left-brain teacher will need to make a conscious effort to better reach the strong right-brain students in the classroom (Connell, 2009).

Ned Herrmann is "Father of brain dominance technology". He drew on the work of Sperry and developed the theory brain dominance where people develop a dominant mode of thinking preference. This can range from an analytical "left Brain" approach to "right brain" approaches involving pattern matching and intuitive understanding. According to Hermann, these preferences are genetically inherited and it affects our underlying cognitive capabilities (Herrmann, N., 1990). How the two systems are inter-connected, with the MI theory is for more future research to be done.

The world's leading thinking styles assessment tool, the Herrmann Brain Dominance Instrument (HBDI) is the assessment at the core of Hermann International's Whole Brain thinking approach. Developed in the 1970's by New Herrmann, then a manager at General Electric, more than thirty years of research and innovation stand behind the validity of the HBDI (Herrmann, 1980).

The basis of Whole Brain thinking and all Herrmann International learning modules, the HBDI teaches you how to communicate with those who think the same as you and those who think differently than you. Once an individual understands his or her thinking style preferences, the door is open to improved teamwork, leadership, customer relationship, creativity, problem solving, and other aspects of personal and interpersonal development. There are copy written short tests, that relate to the multiple intelligences learners, where the right and left brain learners are discovered. This neurological style is interwoven in the Multiple learning identification process. This will be explained later in the methodology section of the thesis.

The Unique Quality of the Visual/Spatial Learner (example)

The past decade has given research valuable information on brain dominances abilities and learning styles. The left hemisphere is to be responsible for temporal, sequential, and analytic functions, whereas the right hemisphere is considered to be the origin of spatial, holistic, and synthetic functions (Bogen, 1969; Dixon, 1983; Levy-Agresti &Sperry, 1968). Different branches of psychology and neurophysiology (Das, Kireby, & Jarman, 1979; Kinsbourne, 1980; Luria, 1966, 1971), agree that both hemispheres need to be integrated for high level of intelligence.

Generally one hemisphere favors one of the other mode of learning (Levy, 1974, 1982). Spatial and sequential dominance are two different metal abilities that affect perceptions. The sequential processor is influenced by time, and less aware of space. The spatial processor is influence with space at the expense of time (Silverman, 1986). Western and Eastern philosophies with cultural expectations, give good examples of these differences. Western thought is sequential, temporal, and analytic; while Eastern thought is spatial and holistic (Bolen, 1979).

This is reflective generally, in the young students as well. These diverse mental organizations appear to be innate. It is balanced by learning and awareness. Instead of trying to remake one or the other style of learning, we need to accept these inherent differences in perception. They are inter-related and inter-connective to a vision of the holistic learner. They enable an exchange of information that forms a complete conception of reality than can be gained by either perspective in isolation (Silverman, 2009).

For example visual/spatial learners perceive the interrelatedness of the whole idea; their learning is holistic and occurs in an all in one fashion. It is not sequential in form, but a process of internal realizations. They are highly curious, and use the creative, imaginative abilities of their perceptions. Unfortunately, the time constraints of public schools, conformity of social interactions, and routine learning activities will turn them off to the school setting. They are likely to be elaborate doodlers, movie buffs, or computer fanatics, while forgetting their homework (Silverman, 1986). They are sometimes called the gifted underachievers. These are children who appear to be gifted to their parent but not to their teachers (Silver, Chitwood, & Waters, 1986) they are often thought of being the "space case", imaginative student.

Introversion of the Visual/Spatial Learner

Silverman, (1986) has found an interesting linkage among IQ, visual-spatial abilities, and introversion. The higher the child's IQ, the greater chance introversion behavior is present.

She found several common characteristics of introverts and spatial learners. Children in both groups are reflective, needs extra time with risk taking, and both groups need time to observe others. They seem bossy or weird in their behavior, which is rejected by others. They tend to be supersensitive, and may withdraw into their own worlds after this type of rejection (Keirsey & Bates, 1978). Introverts gain their energy from themselves and find people very draining. After long periods of time with people, they need time alone in order to regroup. They are very private, and show the world their finished products when they have been done completely (Keirsey & Bates, 1978: Myers, 1962). Like the visual-spatial learning orientation, introversion is an inborn characteristic that remains stable throughout life (Myers, 1962). Most of our western society is extroverted; introverts are not well understood, and well-meaning parents and teachers try to remake these children into extroverts, damaging self-esteem. They need to be respected for who they really are in school and their living environment.

Summary

Multiple Intelligences in all aspects are necessary to understand, before focusing in on one modality. A person is generally a combination of several intelligences, with a right, left, or middle brain dominance in learning styles, needs the expansion of the World Brain theory. There are researchers who stand in opposition to the Whole Brain Theory regardless of the quantitative data used. Many teachers need help through special workshops, mentors, who can guide them in this mode of classroom operations. Many educators have some difficulties with the MI applications in the classroom, while others thrive in this new way to teach. Students are increasing coming to school, with different learning styles. Their test assessments will not tell the complete truth about their learning preferences. New kinds of assessments need to be developed (Gardener, 1986).

For example, the visual/spatial learner, especially in sequential material, and this learner needs extra help in those areas where he/she are the weakest. Each child has dominance and a weakness in their learning potential. It is important to activate the weakness and integrate both hemispheres in unison. Being too much to the left causes problems to the learning potential of the student, or being too much to the right, also causes problems for the student. The learner needs to seek brain processing balance to be an effective student. A student's innate preference, or learning comfort zone, can be a problem for the balanced learner.

This is where the identification of the MI intelligence with right brain or left-brain orientation becomes a valuable diagnostic tool for the teacher. There are methods within the MI theory that facilitates this balance needed for learning. One of the unique students is the Visual/Spatial Modality are all unique individuals, but in the classroom, this is not recognized by the curriculum's focus, here in the west. A balance, healthy mind is necessary for the successful student (Connell, 2009). We need to celebrate our differences, and our individuality.

"For example, the visual/spatial learners have been badly wounded in the traditional system. They have been made to feel stupid, lazy, defiant, and unworthy, all because their unique learning style has not been fully understood and appreciated (Silverman, 2008)". How this is done through methodology is the subject of the next chapter. It will describe the participants, instrumentation, distribution, limitations, and delimitations of the study.

CHAPTER THREE

METHODOLOGY

The purpose of this study was to understand the Whole Brain Theory, with the Multiple Learning Intelligences and Brain Dominance findings. The preference surveys did help identify a learners dominant intelligences and Brain Processing. This chapter describes the research design, the population, sampling procedures, instrumentation, data collection procedures, limitations and summary.

Participants

The projected participants of this study were ten diverse adults who were not born in United States, eight public school secondary teachers, two public school administrators and fifty secondary students. The diverse adults were from India, Tibet, Mexico, Brazil, and China. The students came from the Hemet Unified School District, and were in the researcher's ceramics and multimedia classes.

The group of participants selected consisted of a convenience sample. A convenience sample is a sample where the study participants are selected at the convenience of the researcher. In choosing a convenience sample, the research made no attempt, or only a limited attempt, to insure that this sample is an accurate representation of some larger group or population.

Instrumentation

The surveys were created by the researcher. Prior to constructing the surveys, the researcher conducted a literature review in order to gain an understanding of the current state of knowledge pertaining to the Whole Brain Theory, Multiple Intelligences, and Brain Dominance. From this the researcher determined which data collection methods had been used previously for similar research and the findings from the data analyses in previously conducted research. The researcher found that many of the professional surveys, used by business corporations required prohibitive amounts of funds for their use because of copyright regulations. Examples of these copyrighted and expensive tests were Ned Hermann's Whole Brain Instrument and the Myers Briggs test.

the validity of the survey responses. Therefore, the researcher rewrote the questions until they were considered clear and to-the-point. Next, the researcher determined the question type most relevant to the research questions. She then organized the format of the surveys and received input from others that the survey would be clear to potential respondents. No pilot testing was conducted.

1. Appendix A has the Brain dominance test used for the older adult learner. It has A series of 50 questions, with an answer key and assessment. It is hand corrected by the researcher, and not computerized. The participates are not named, but their age, career, education level, culture, and other facts are on the survey notes. The survey sought to find the brain dominance of a particular learner.

2. Appendix B has a sixteen question survey, with nine sections focused on the diverse adult learners, and secondary high school students. It is not for teachers who have different preferences than the non-educator. The surveys contained the nine intelligences of the MI theory of Howard Gardner. It has nine sections with certain percentages that are displayed on a colored scale. It is self-corrected by the researcher, as well. The colored scale tells what MI intelligence the learner prefers to use.

3. Appendix C is a MI survey only for the classroom educator, with a data sheet as well. It has some extra intelligences that relates only to the classroom teacher or administrator. The intelligences are in a different sequence than appendix B, and has ten questions in each of the nine sections of the survey. It is also self corrected by the researcher, with specific notes about the educators career status, location of life, family, culture, and gender. There is a colored graph with preferences intelligences as well.

Distribution

The survey papers were given to some of the participates at different times. The secondary surveys were done in a multimedia art class, and a ceramics lab taught by the researcher, in the fall of 2009 in Hemet, California. The teachers completed the surveys we at different times, or when it was convenient. There was constant supervision of the participates while taking the surveys. The ten diverse cultural participates group were given at different times through-out the year. The process took a year to complete. The surveys were not computerized and had to be corrected by hand. It included colored graphs to visually illustrate the survey findings.

Surveys were completed by hand. Computers were not always available, and some of the multicultural group did not have the computer literacy to use them. Many of the multicultural diverse people needed the researchers help in reading and understanding the material. However, no assistance was given in guiding participants to any specific answers; answers are the respondents' own answers. The data papers are kept without the main tests in a separate pile, in order to ensure confidentiality. These two surveys of the Brain Dominance and Multiple intelligences were the most important for the individual for the individual learner at all levels.

Methodological Assumptions

The surveys were assumed to accurately test for preferred intelligences and Brain Dominances within the targeted groups. The surveys were not tested in an experimental lab, the researcher could only assume that the surveys were effective as a diagnostic tool.

Limitations

The high schools were on a restrictive schedule, and they were not always open to the possibility of outside testing procedures. Teacher and student ratio was subject to change as were the inclusion of special schedules for special events. Therefore the reseacher used secondary classes, which were available during her long-term substitute teaching assignments. The diverse multicultural adult learners took the surveys at different times during the year of 2009. The surveys were created from the researcher and other cited surveys from Internet sources. The surveys do not have scientific accountability from a panel of educational experts.

Delimitations

Delimitations to this study were as follows:

1. The various surveys were designed to accommodate the differences between the secondary student, diverse adult learner, and public school educator.
2. There was little scientific assessment for this field of inquiry presently.
3. Two of the scientific qualitative surveys of Ned Herrmann (2003) and the Brain Dominance are not available without cost to the public sector. Myers Briggs personality test was in the same category, along with copy right issues.

Summary

The diagnostic tools were two survey tests created by the researcher for several Internet sources with an impartial scoring systems. Fifty secondary students were chosen to take the survey test of the Multiple Intelligences and the Brain Hemispheric Dominance survey. Eight public school educators and two administrators took the survey as well. There were also ten multicultural adult learners in the group for the surveys. The diverse adult learners were from India, Brazil, China, and Mexico. They had a combination of education levels and a gender break down for clarification of preference levels. Adults seem to be more aware than the secondary learner of their preferences, especially the adult educator. When the tests were completed, the data sheet result was used for assessments.

From the data collected by the researcher, the surveys were analyzed. This data was put on a graph for an analysis by the researcher. In Chapter Four the tables will show some of the distribution breakdown of these differences.

CHAPTER FOUR

FINDINGS

The purpose of this study was to determine if the Whole Brain Theory has merit to expand the teacher's knowledge of how a student learns, and processes information. Individual curriculum designs can be created from such data. The two categories of the most importance to the whole brain theory is the Multiple Intelligence Theory, and the Brain Dominance theory, developed by neuroscientists.

Background and Setting

As a method of researching, whether or not educators were aware of their own preferences, predominant Brain Dominance, and learning intelligences, eight public school teachers, including two administrators, ten adult multicultural adults, and fifty secondary students were surveyed to discover their brain learning functions. The survey was gathered through the researcher's network online, public school classrooms, and in multicultural community groups. The adult learners and teachers, who participated in the research study were from the San Bernardino, Riverside, Los Angeles, and San Diego counties.

Students

The secondary students were teen learners at the secondary level. They were enrolled in the researcher's Art multimedia programs, ceramics, and visual design courses at the high school level. Many of these students were right-brain dominant, visual/spatial, kinesthetic learners before entering the class, because of choosing the creative art elective. The diagnostic tools showed this preference to be true when taking the surveys. The subject matter does inform teachers what the learning preferences, brain dominance, and intelligences, in many instances. There are exceptions to the rule, on a larger scale of teen learners. Table 4.1 shows this preference scale. There were also more males enrolled in these classes than females. Out of classes of fifty students, the majority of the preferred intelligences were right-brain dominant, visual/spatial, kinesthetic, interpersonal, musical learners. They learn best with music from the I pods, group social interactions, and physically walking around

was a need for group collaboration, and a sharing of ideas. The classes were majority of Hispanic ethnic origins, and of low economic levels of family income. Income directly affects the availability of educational enrichment activities, and healthy foods for the growing child and adult. Certain low income cultures, tend to be more right brain processes, do not discipline their children the same as Left-brain parents. This is the same of the right brain teacher as well (Connell, 2009, pp.3).

All the educators held higher degrees, credentials, administrative credentials, and were high school graduates in the American Public Schools. The educators were experienced in teaching in the classroom. The researcher tried to find educators who had been credentialed, for at least six years, and have been involved in some kind of administrative duties. The two administrators were working for over ten years, and one male supervisor was retired, and the other female was working as a vice principal in a middle school.

The other adult learners were born in different regions of the world, and had a high school diploma in the home country, and in the USA. The researcher avoided using persons who did not have a high school or GED diploma here in America.

Analysis of Selected Findings

Based on the data collected, the Whole Brain Learning Theory is fast becoming a major focus in the future learning environments. All of the participants in the program except the educators had little knowledge of the process until the surveys were given. About 5 % of secondary students had been exposed to the brain dominances from their other teachers in the schools, 50 % or half of the educators were more aware of the MI theories, than Brain dominances. None of the diverse multicultural adult learners had any knowledge of such a learning procedure. See the below charts for more informative data.

Table 4.1 Group comparisons about the Whole Brain Learning Theory.

Say YES if you have had some exposure to your Brain Dominance or MI intelligences	Response Frequency	Response Count
Participates were questioned before they started theSurveys. n=70	100 %	70
Fifty secondary students out of seventy participates n=50	45 %	45
Ten educators out of seventy participates n=10	90 %	9
Ten multicultural diverse learners out of seventy Participates. n=10	0%	0
Say YES if you feel you want to know HOW you Learn by the Whole Brain Learning Theory		
Fifty secondary students out of seventy participates n=50	90 %	48
Ten educators out of seventy participates n=10	100%	10
Ten multicultural adult learners out of seventy participates. n=10	100%	10

Educators Among the ten educators, eight educators said they had known about the research, but felt it had little impact on their teaching style. Only two of the educators felt it was important enough to implement it in their classroom. The majority of the educators felt

It matter for the learning success of the students, but it was too time consuming to implement. The majority of the educators felt it should be part of the Resource, SDC, and remedial teachers to use in their diagnostic procedures. About three out of ten of the teachers did not like the concept at all, and did not want to take the class time to implement the program. All of the educators felt it was a good idea but was not practical. The majority of the educators felt they would have to have expertise training and supervision of such a program.

The secondary students were of another opinion. Over 80 % felt that knowing their learning styles might help them perform better on student assessments, and standardized testing. Over 90 % felt they might learn better if the teachers would accommodate their learning styles. Most of the left-brain learners were not concerned, because most of these students were receiving adequate grades. Why? because the curriculum design favors the left-brain processor.

Other Adult Learners

Over ten adult learners felt it was important to them to understand how they processed their learning information. This information would help them in their communication, and relationships at home, work, and career aspirations. This individualized attention would be a positive addition to their learning process. They were open to any information that would help them function more efficiently in their lives. Below is some extra information pertaining to gender assessment, and ethnicity

Table 4.2 Language acquisition and brain dominance

Groups & Subjects	Language spoken at Home (Spanish)	Right brain	Left Brain
Secondary Students 50/70			**English only**
Multimedia subject	15 out of 25 has Spanish at home	15	10
Ceramics subject	10 out of 25 has Spanish at home	10	15
Multicultural Adults n=10	2 out of 10 Spanish speaking	2	8
Educators n=10	3 out of 10 Spanish speaking	3	7
Total 30 out of 70 are right Brain dominant		30 are bilingual	
Total 40 out of 70 are English only			40 are English only

What this chart is saying that among the secondary students, educators, and multicultural adults who have had a Spanish background culturally, or born with parents who speak the language at home, their preference is right-brain dominant 42% in most of the cases. The MI intelligences vary somewhat in what career or choice of a career they might be doing. Language seems to be the key factor in the brain dominance, MI theory is govern more by what they are doing in life, career, studies, and education

Table 4.3 Educational level and Brain Dominance n=20

Multicultural Adult learner n=20 out of 70 And Teacher educational levels and cultures.	Right	Left
1 Hispanic pre school teacher adult learner (F) College	X	
1 Hispanic teacher in RSP (M) College	X	
1 Primary teacher in Elementary (F) College	X	
1 Hispanic Gardner (M) High School	X	
1 African American Musician (M) High school grad	X	
1 African American Administrator (F) College	X	
1 Brazilian American musician (M) High schoolgrad.	X	
1 Brazilian American Dancer (F) High school grad	X	
1 Brasilian American Principal (M) College grad		X
1 Bangledesh American (M) College		X
1 Palestinian American (M) High School grad		X
1 Tibetan Rinpoche (M)—Dharma College grad	X	
1 Bangledesh Orthopedic docter (M) Western College gr		X
1 Chinese Secretary (F) Medical—high school grad		X
1 Chinese teacher (M) education in China College		X
1 White (M) Therapist College graduate	X	
1 White (F) Principal teacher and administration		X
1 White (F) Retired Spanish teacher, College grad.		X
1 White (M) Administrator College grad. Retired.		X
1 White (F) Finnish Teacher Aide High school grad		X

These adult educators, administrators, and adult learners have dominate Brain Learning preferences. The researcher data says it is important to start with Brain Dominance first, and to find out more information about the learner's processes with MI diagnostic surveys. The consistency of the Hispanic learner regardless of how much college education they have, seems to be affected by their language acquisition, and culture. The rest of the diverse persons are affected by education, culture, language, and career choices. There are exceptions to the rule only a few times. Education level, culture, and parental background seems to affect the brain dominance of the participates.

Table 4.4 Gender and Education

Groups	Males	Females	Gender Effect on Educational Goals
Multimedia design class. Ages 16-18 Ceramics Ages 16-18	15 15	10 10	1 % Hispanic 5%
Adult learners diverse Hispanic 1 high school graduate age 42 1 Hispanic preschool teacher age 32 1 Hispanic RSP teacher age 33 1 Hispanic Primary teacher age 27	1 1 	 1 1	45% 30% 30% 40%
1 Afro-American—high school age 42 1 Afro-American college Age 52 1 Afro-Brazilian High school, age 35 1 Afro-Brazilian High school age 27 1 Afro-Brazilian teacher College age 57	1 1 	 1 1 1	70% 65% 50% 35% 60%
1 Bangladesh Business college age 67 1 Bangladesh Doctor College age 57 1 Palestine-American HS grad age 62 1 Tibetan Lama College age 35	1 1 1 1		65% 60% 75 % 50%
1 Chinese Secretary College age 37 1 Chinese teacher College age 45	 1	1 	25% 40%
1 White Therapist College age 37 1 White Finnish teach aide HS age 58	1 	 1	10% 60%
1 White Principal supervision age 55 1 Spanish Teacher College age 69 1 white Administrator retired age 72 Total	 1 11	1 1 9	50% 80% 50%

The gender issue was not a prime importance here in American among the secondary students. The older the adult learner was, and their ethnicity did affect their motivation to seek educational goals. The diverse adult learners felt from their cultural roots that they was a gender gap caused by the roles men and woman play. Western education seems to be the force of equality. It does seem that to be the deciding factors. Woman are more conditioned to be right-brain processors from these traditional societies than here in the west. Again a western education, which is left-brain dominate helps alleviate the gender gap. Most of the participates felt in their own country of their birth, there are more obstacles for a woman than a man, to gain an educational power position, than for men. Alan Ornstein states: "Title IX of the 1972 Education Amendments to the Civil Rights Act and the Women's Educational Equity Act of 1974 (WEEA) prohibited discrimination against women in federally aided education programs. Trends emerging from this legislation increased the amount of women involved in Mathematics, science, athletics, and technology programs and careers" (Ornstein, 2008pp.258). This is part of American legislation, and many other countries of the world do not have such laws regarded gender discrimination.

Summary

These surveys were conducted to evaluate, and group different learners in different modes of learning preferences. The Whole Brain Theory needs hard, concrete data that rests on the quality of the surveys given. The administrators, educators, felt the implementation of the surveys, was too time consuming, and impractical for the public school system. They also felt it would take more funding, teacher training, with curriculum design reform to make it happen. So many of the administrators, teachers were left-brain orientated with little vision as the right-brain visionary. The structure of the state system of education has not focused on the individual learner, and there is a movement towards a massive curriculum design for all public schools in the nation (Ornstein, 2008 pp.358).

While this may be some of the feelings of the educators, the adult, secondary learners felt the information had a positive influence on their learning. They wanted to know how they learned, and why certain subjects were difficult for them to achieve success. Thus there seems to be an opposite of view here between the teacher, administration, and the learner.

With all the complexities of today's educational structure, it still is the individual teacher who could use this data in his/her classroom to help all students learn better. It is within the power of the individual teacher to implement the data if they wish to.

In Chapter Five there will be a Summary of the Chapters, with a conclusion and recommendations.

CHAPTER FIVE

SUMMARY, CONCLUSIONS, AND RECOMMENDATIONS

Factual summary of the findings

Within the previous Chapter Four, there are several Brain Dominance surveys with MI intelligence tests for the 50 secondary students, 10 diverse multicultural students, 8 educators, and two administrators, which illustrates how various persons process information or learn. The validity of the surveys were quite revealing especially in the field of the Spanish, and language acquisition. It does affect the brain preferences through cultural interactions. Also the more a student has a left-brain western education, the more left-brain the student becomes.

In Table 4.1 we dealt with the group comparisons about the Whole Brain Theory. The researcher wanted to know if the participants have had any exposure to the MI intelligence, Brain Dominance theories, or the Whole Brain Theory in general. The researcher questioned each participant in the survey. In the secondary section of students, 100 % of the students were asked if they had any idea about how they learned, or the Whole Brain theory, and surprising enough many of the students 45 out of 50 students had some idea of what it meant. The researcher asked them where they received their input, and the answer was from their internet experience. Their classroom teacher did not give the secondary students any information about the process. Over 90% wanted to know how they learned, and felt it would help them process information they were struggling with.

In the educator's group were asked the same question as the secondary students, and only one math educated teacher from another country (Chinese) had not heard of the theories. The rest of the teachers had studied some MI theories, and a little of the Brain Dominance theories. The educator group all felt that this Whole Brain theory might be a help with the struggling learner at all grades and subjects. Most of the educators and especially the administrators felt the practical application could be a huge task to implement. Then the multicultural diverse learners had no idea what the researcher was speaking about, and wanted to know more how they learn. Many of the participants were very curious about the findings of the tests, and how it affected their learning styles. It seems the findings of the neuroscientific community was not high priority on the training of teachers.

It seem from all the findings of bi-lingual students of Spanish ancestry and traditions all register right-brain dominate in their learning processing. As long as they still spoke their native language Spanish, regardless of their educational level, the group still register right-brain. The participants where taken from a small area. The less they spoke Spanish in their culture, the more left-brain they became. So the researcher feels that language acquisition, especially Spanish,is a determine factor in brain processing. In the case of the Spanish-speaker, their culture had to be completely wiped out of them to become a dominant left-brain processor. When the Spanish speaker, balanced their culture with the west, most of the time they became a balanced learner. This is the goal of the Whole Brain theory to seek a balance of our brain dominances.

In the table 4.3 Educational level and Brain Dominance, n=20, there was a contrast between cultures, educational levels, and languages. According to this graph, the adults who were educated in the western cultures indicated a strong left-brain preference, and the adults in certain Asian countries were varied and mixed, but still right-brain dominant. Western education is left-brain dominate curriculum design; unless there is reform of the curriculum emphasize it will remain so.

In table 4.4 the gender issue does not seem to be the prime issue, but the cultural expectations of the gender is. When a person, male or female does not have a western type of education, they remain right-brain dominate. This starts at a young age, mainly at birth. Each brain dominance gives the whole brain a preference or an ability to acquire information. Children may not establish brain dominance until they are about five years old, and it is mainly right-brain preference. Other studies suggest that children continue to develop their brain preference until they reach puberty (Luria, 1966).

Conclusion

The researcher concludes that more research in the field of multicultural affects on Brain Dominance and MI intelligences needs to be done. Culture, educational levels does affect the Brain Dominance of the developing child into an adult. Certain languages other than Spanish, carries certain unconscious energy, which affects the brain activity. Every culture, language, and traditions carries certain unspoken behaviors that affect the behavior of each learner in the community. We need to explore how our education system is affecting our students, and communities. Education of both Brain hemispheres, right/left and whole brain curriculum need to be put into the curriculum design.

Recommendations

From my findings and research the work of Roger Sperry and his bi-sector of the Brain, neuroscientists Brain dominance, MI intelligences, and the World Brain Theory fits like an interwoven puzzle. A learner's culture, native language, traditions, genes, career, affect a learner's ability to learn. Education seems to be the deciding factor in changing Brain dominance, and MI intelligences preferences. There are all kinds of education in the world, not just reading, writing, and information acquisitions. Individualized portfolios, student and teachers of their learning preferences can be used to design an individual or a group curriculum design. A verbal, written and project assessments for assessment tools can be used. Students should be exposed to multiple assessment methods (Jensen, 1998). To most educators why does this matter in education? We as human beings are different in the way we process information, and to understand why we learn differently from our friends, helps liberate a child, secondary students, and adults from the frustration of not fitting in with the norm.

These above suggestions can be used at the secondary level and adult learning environment to stimulate the brain based learning environment. At the public school level at North Carolina Public Schools, there is a "Balance Curriculum, Education for the Whole Child". You can access it at the

Public schools of North Carolina online or from Michael E. Ward, State Superintendent 301 N. Wilmington Street, Raleigh, North Carolina 27601-2825, www.ncpublicschools, org. This is one of their quotes in the curriculum: "Learning is change. It is change in our selves because it is change in the brain. Thus the art of teaching must be the art of changing the Brain" (Zull. 2002).

Presently there is a movement call the Mind, Brain, & Education which links Biology, Neuroscience, & Educational Practice, which comes from the Harvard Graduate School in Boston Massachusetts. There are so many MBE doctoral students and science persons involve in this cognitive neuroscience research, that no longer can we as educators ignore the part the brain plays in our education. Without the education researchers, the mission of MBE, is to train students who will build that bridge between the lab and the classroom. This is still a young field. The more research and experimentation is needed to form lasting results of the Mind, Brain, Education or the Whole Mind or Brain Learning Theory in Education. At least educators need to be aware of the research, which is an on going process (Hanna, 2005, pp.8).

APPENDIX: A

Right/Left Brain Preference Survey

Whole Brain Preference Test

Age:
Culture or nationality:
Date:
Location:
Level of education

Right/Left Dominance Processing.

This is a printable survey to give to participates to determine Brain Dominance. Print out the test, and have the students take another sheet of paper; add the class, nationality, language, and age. Every time you read a description or characteristics that applies to you, then write the number on a blank sheet of paper. Whatever the highest number will give you the dominant brain preference that you function with (Angel Fire, 2009, Education World, 2010, Intelligent Inc., 2000).

Part I (Quiz)

1. I constantly look a clock or wear a watch.
2. I keep a journal or diary of my thoughts.
3. I believe there is a either right or wrong way to do everything.
4. I find it hard to follow direction precisely.
5. The expression Life is just a bowl of cherries makes no sense to me.
6. I frequently change my plans and find that sticking to a schedule is boring.
7. I think it's easier to draw a map than tell someone how to get somewhere.
8. To find a lost item, I try to picture it in my head where I last saw it.
9. I frequently let my emotions guide me.
10. I learn math with ease.
11. I'd read the directions before assembling something.
12. People tell me I am always late getting places.
13. People tell me that I am psychic.
14. When someone asks me a question, I turn my head to the left.
15. I need to set goals for myself to keep me on track.
16. If I have a tough decision to make, I write down the pros and cons.
17. I would make a good detective.
18. I learn music with ease.
19. To solve a problem, I think of similar problems I have solved in the past.
20. I use a lot of hand gestures.
21. If someone asks me a question, I turn my head to the right.
22. I believe there are two ways to look at almost everything.
23. I have the ability to tell if people are lying or guilty of something, just by looking at them.
24. I keep a to do list.
25. I am able to thoroughly explain my opinions in words.

26. In a debate, I am objective and look at the facts before forming an opinion.
27. I've considered becoming a poet, an architect, or a dancer.
28. I always lose track of time.
29. When trying to remember a name I forgot, I'd recite the alphabet until I remembered it.
30. I like to draw.
31. When I'm confused, I usually go with my gut instinct.
32. I have considered becoming a lawyer, journalist, or doctor.
33. I am better remembering faces than names.
34. I am an organized person.
35. I like imaginative fantasy stories.
36. I like to debate issues.
37. I like open-ended assignments.
38. I remember things through words.
39. I like working with my hands doing creative crafts.
40. I think very serious thoughts.
41. I daydream at least once a day.
42. I like to learn through experimentation.
43. I am involved in dramatic performances.
44. I must have a place for everything.
45. When I take an exam, I like to do the written part better.
46. When I am doing a dance step, it is easier if I see the whole dance first.
47. I doodle when I am bore.
48. I am able to think by walking around.
49. In Math I am able to express in words how I did the solution.
50. In a magazine, I look at the main titles before reading the article.

Now take the answer Key and write down the numbers that are most like your behavior. Then check to see what hemisphere you are dominant in.

Key

1. L	11. L	21. L	31. R	41. R
2. L	12. R	22. R	32. L	42. L
3. L	13. R	23. R	33. R	43. R
4. R	14. R	24. L	34. L	44. L
5. L	15. L	25. L	35. R	45. L
6. R	16 L	26. L	36. L	46. R
7. R	17. L	27. R	37. R	47. R
8. L	18. R	28. R	38. L	48. R
9. R	19. R	29. L	39. R	49. L
10. L	20. R	30 R	40. L	50. L

Dominant brain preference is Left _____, Right _____.
    You are a _____ (Right, Left, Whole brain thinker and processor, from this survey.

Left Side of the Brain

- Processes verbal, abstract, analytical information in a linear, sequential manner.
- Looks a differences and contrasts, seeing small signs that represent the whole,
- Concerns itself with reasoning abilities such as math and language.

Right Side of the Brain

- Processes non-verbal, concrete, and spatial information,
- Looks at similarities in patterns, forming a whole picture, and processing parts in relationship to The Whole,
- Concerns itself with artistic abilities such as music and graphics.

APPENDIX: B

Multiple Subjects Survey for Students

Multiple Intelligences Survey

Complied by Whole Brain Theory
(BGFL, 2002; Chapman.2002; Literacy works, 2003; McKenzie, 1999)

Part I

Complete each section by checking the box that you feel accurately describes you.

Section 1 (Nature smart)
Nature Intelligence Strength

- ☐ I enjoy categorizing things by common traits.
- ☐ Ecological issues are important to me.
- ☐ Classification helps me make sense of new data.
- ☐ I enjoy working in a garden.
- ☐ I believe preserving our National Parks is important.
- ☐ Putting things in hierarchies makes sense to me.
- ☐ Animals are important in my life.
- ☐ My home has a recycling system in place.
- ☐ I enjoy studying biology, botany and/ or zoology.
- ☐ I pick up on subtle differences in meaning.
- ☐ Pollution makes me angry.
- ☐ I enjoy being outdoors when I learn.
- ☐ I can recognize and name different types of birds, trees and plants.
- ☐ I like films or videos on wild life, nature, and survival techniques.
- ☐ I like to go camping, hiking,and mountain living.
- ☐ I like to have many house plants, and gardens around me.
- ☐ Total is _____

Section 2 (Music Smart)
Musical Intelligence Strength

- ☐ I easily pick up on patterns
- ☐ I focus in on noise and sounds
- ☐ Moving to a beat is easy for me.
- ☐ I enjoy making music.
- ☐ I respond to the cadence of poetry.
- ☐ I remember things by putting them in a rhyme.
- ☐ Concentration is difficult for me if there is background noise.
- ☐ Listening to sounds in nature can be very relaxing.
- ☐ Musicals are more engaging to me than dramatic plays.
- ☐ Remembering song lyrics is easy for me.
- ☐ I can play or used to play, a musical instrument.
- ☐ I pick up new dance steps easily.
- ☐ Life seems empty without music.
- ☐ I often connect a piece of music with some event in my life.
- ☐ I like to hum, whistle and sing in the shower or when I am alone.
- ☐ When bored, I will beat on my desk, or use pencils.
- ☐ Total is _____

Notes:

Section Three (Number Smart)
Logical Intelligence Strength

- ☐ I am known for being neat and orderly.
- ☐ Step by step directions are a big help.
- ☐ Problem solving comes easily to me.
- ☐ I get easily frustrated with disorganized people.
- ☐ I can complete calculations quickly in my head.
- ☐ Logical puzzles are fun.
- ☐ I can't begin an assignment until I have all the parts in the whole.
- ☐ Structure is a good thing.
- ☐ I enjoy troubleshooting something that isn't working properly
- ☐ Things have to make sense to me or I am dissatisfied.
- ☐ I am good at mathematical problems and using numbers.
- ☐ I can take things apart and put them back together easily.
- ☐ I often develop equations to describe relationships and or to explain my observations.
- ☐ I often see mathematical rations in the world around me.
- ☐ Math is generally my favorite subject.
- ☐ I like to think about numerical issues and examine statistics.
- ☐ Total is _____.

Notes:

Section Four (Spiritual Smart)
Existential Intelligence Strength, Spiritual Strength or Metaphysical

- ☐ I need to explore the large picture of things.
- ☐ I enjoy questions about life and the universe.
- ☐ Religion and spiritual paths are important to me.
- ☐ I enjoy viewing visionary artwork.
- ☐ I enjoy listening to meditative spiritual music.
- ☐ I enjoy comparative religions.
- ☐ I like indigenous native spiritual rituals.
- ☐ Relaxation and meditation exercises are rewarding to me.
- ☐ I like traveling to visit inspiring places, or spiritual vortexes.
- ☐ I enjoy reading global philosophers
- ☐ I like learning about consciousness studies.
- ☐ Learning new things is easier when I see their real world applications.
- ☐ I like cosmology principles, theoritical scientific physics and chemistry findings.
- ☐ I like paranormal experimental studies.
- ☐ Esoteric global metaphysical studies interest me.
- ☐ It is important for me to feel connected to people, cultures, ideas, and beliefs.
- ☐ Total is _____.

Notes:

Section Five (People Smart)
Interpersonal Intelligence and Strengths

- ☐ I learn best interacting with others.
- ☐ I enjoy informal chat and serious discussion.
- ☐ The more the merrier.
- ☐ I often serve as a leader among peers and colleagues.
- ☐ I value relationships more than ideas or accomplishments.
- ☐ Study groups are very productive for me.
- ☐ I am a team player.
- ☐ Friends are important to me.
- ☐ I belong to more than three clubs or organizations.
- ☐ I dislike working alone.
- ☐ I respond to all people enthusiastically, free of bias or prejudice.
- ☐ I enjoy new and diverse kinds of social situations.
- ☐ I am quick to sense in others dishonesty and desire to control me.
- ☐ I feel safe when I am with strangers.
- ☐ I can sort out arguments between friends.
- ☐ I am sensitive to the moods and feelings of others.
- ☐ Total is _____

Notes:

Section Six (Body Smart)
Kinesthetic Intelligence and Strength

☐ I learn by doing
☐ I enjoy making things with my hands.
☐ Sports are a part of my life.
☐ I use gestures and non-verbal cues when I communicate.
☐ Demonstrating is better than explaining.
☐ I love to dance.
☐ I like working with tools.
☐ Inactivity can make me more tired than being very busy.
☐ Hands-on activities are fun.
☐ I live an active lifestyle.
☐ I have problems sitting still quietly.
☐ I enjoy working on computers.
☐ I belong to a gym and take aerobic classes.
☐ I feel really good about being physically fit.
☐ I watch sports on television or go to sports games.
☐ My family is involved in a team sport activities.
☐ Total _____

Notes:

Section Seven (word smart)
Linguistic Intelligence

- ☐ Foreign languages interest me.
- ☐ I enjoy reading books, magazines and web sites.
- ☐ I keep a diary or journal, and write in it, at least once a week.
- ☐ Word puzzles like crosswords or jumbles are enjoyable.
- ☐ Games like scramble are fun to me.
- ☐ Taking notes helps me remember and understand.
- ☐ I like writing stories, and research papers.
- ☐ I contact friends through letters and or emails.
- ☐ It is easy for me to explain my ideas to others, and text on my cell phone a lot.
- ☐ I write for pleasure.
- ☐ Puns, anagrams and spoonerisms are fun.
- ☐ I enjoy public speaking and participating in debates.
- ☐ I have been involved in another foreign language other than my own.
- ☐ I enjoy multi-culturist activities.
- ☐ I read a lot for pleasure, novels, and poetry.
- ☐ I enjoy watching classical dramas, on stage or in films.
- ☐ Total _____

Notes:

Section Eight (Self Development smart)
Intrapersonal Intelligence

- ☐ My mental and emotional attitude affects how I learn.
- ☐ I like to be involved in causes that help others.
- ☐ I am keenly aware of my moral and ethical beliefs.
- ☐ I learn best when I have an emotional attachment to the subject.
- ☐ Fairness is important to me.
- ☐ Working alone can be just as productive as working in a group.
- ☐ I need to know why I should do something before I agree to do it.
- ☐ When I believe in something I give more effort towards it.
- ☐ I am willing to protest or sign a petition to right a wrong.
- ☐ I like working and thinking on my own and quietly.
- ☐ I am an independent thinker. I know my own mind.
- ☐ I can use many different methods to describe myself
- ☐ I enjoy self development courses, and meditation activities.
- ☐ I function best in a non-distracted working environment.
- ☐ I like to sit quietly and reflect on my inner feelings.
- ☐ I like to stay in touch with my moods, and have no problems identifying them.
- ☐ Total _____

Notes:

Section 9 (Visual smart)
Visual/Spatial Intelligence

- ☐ I can visualize ideas in my mind.
- ☐ Rearranging a room and redecorating are fun for me.
- ☐ I enjoy creating my own works of art.
- ☐ I remember better using graphic organizers.
- ☐ I enjoy all kinds of entertainment media.
- ☐ Charts, graphs and tables help me interpret data.
- ☐ A music video can make me more interested in a song.
- ☐ I can recall things as mental pictures.
- ☐ I am good at reading maps and blueprints.
- ☐ Three dimensional puzzles are fun.
- ☐ I do not get lost easily and can orient myself with either maps or landmarks.
- ☐ I have the ability to represent what I see by drawing and painting.
- ☐ I can easily duplicate color, form, shading, and texture in my work.
- ☐ I am able to visualize a image and hold it for a long time to duplicate.
- ☐ I daydream a lot with multiple images.
- ☐ I have a vivid dream life.
- ☐ Total _____.

Notes:

Part II

Now carry forward your total from each section and multiply by 10 below.

Section	Total Forward	Multiply	Score
1		X10	
2		X10	
3		X10	
4		X10	
5		X10	
6		X10	
7		X10	
8		X10	
9		X10	

Notes:

Part III

Now plot your scores on the bar graph provided.

100									
90									
80									
70									
60									
50									
40									
30									
20									
10									
0									
Section	1	2	3	4	5	6	7	8	9

Section 1—This reflects your Naturalist strength

Section 2—This suggests your Musical strength.

Section 3—This indicates your Logical strength.

Section 4—This illustrates your Existential or Metaphysical strength.

Section 5—This shows your Interpersonal strength.

Section 6—This tells your Kinesthetic strength.

Section 7—This indicates your Verbal strength.

Section 8—This reflects your intrapersonal strength.

Section 9—This suggest your Visual/ Spatial strength.

APPENDIX: C

Multiple Intelligences Teacher Inventory

Multiple Intelligences Teacher Inventory

Place a check in all box that best describe you.

(Jeffcoweb.jeffco.k-12.co.us/)

LINGUISTIC Section 1

☐ I really enjoy books.

☐ I hear words in my head before I write, read or speak them.

☐ I remember more when I listen to the radio or an audiocassette than from television or films.

☐ I enjoy word game such as crossword puzzles, Scrabble, anagrama, or Password.

☐ I like puns, tongue twisters, nonsense rhymes, and double meanings.

☐ English, Social Studies, and History were easier subjects for me than Science and Math.

☐ When I'm driving I like to read the billboards and signs, and notice them more than the scenery along the road.

☐ I often refer to things I have read or heard in conversations.

☐ People often ask me the meaning of words.

☐ I have written something recently that I was proud of, or that was published or recognized.

☐ Total Linguistic boxes checked. _____

LOGICAL Section 2

☐ I can quickly and easily compute numbers in my head (example: double or triple a cooking recipe or carpentry measurement without having to write it on paper).

☐ I enjoy Math and Science in school.

☐ I like solving brainteasers, logical games and other strategy games such as chess/checkers.

☐ I like to set up what if experiments (example: "What if I fertilized my plants twice as often?"

☐ I wonder about how some things work and keep up to date on new scientific developments and discoveries.

☐ I look for structure, patterns, sequences, or logical order.

☐ I believe that there is a rational explanation for almost everything.

☐ I can think in abstract, clear, imageless concepts.

☐ I can find logical flows in things people say and do at work or home.

☐ I feel more comfortable when things have been quantified, measured, categorized, or analyzed in some way.

☐ Total Logical boxed checked. _____

SPATIAL Section 3

☐ When I close my eyes, I can see clear visual images.

☐ I am responsive to color.

☐ I often use a camcorder or camera to record my surroundings.

☐ I enjoy visual puzzles such as mazes, jigsaw puzzles, 3-D images.

☐ I have vivid dreams at night.
☐ I navigate well in unfamiliar places.
☐ I often draw or doodle
☐ Geometry was easier than Alegbra.
☐ I can imagine what something would look like from a bird's eye view.
☐ I prefer reading books, newspaper, magazines, etc. that have many illustrations.
☐ Total Spatial boxed checked _____

BODILY-KINESTHETIC Section 4

☐ I take Part in at least on sport or physical activity regularly.
☐ I find it difficult to sit still for long periods of time.
☐ I like working with my hands such as in crafts or computers.
☐ I frequently get insights or ideas when I am involved in physical activities, such as walking swimming or jogging.
☐ I enjoy spending my free time outside.
☐ I ten to use gestures and other body language when engaged conversations.
☐ I need to touch or hold objects to learn more about them.
☐ I enjoy dare devil activities such as parachuting, bung jumping, and thrilling amusement rides.
☐ I am well-coordinated.
☐ To learn new skills, I need to practice them rather than simple read about them or watch them being performed.
☐ Total Bodily Kinesthetic boxes checked.

MUSICAL Section 5

☐ I have a nice singing voice.
☐ I know when musical notes are off-key.
☐ I often listen to musical selections on radio, records, tapes, CDS, etc.
☐ I play an instrument
☐ My life would be less dynamic without music.
☐ I often have a tune running through my mind during the day.
☐ I can keep time to a piece of music.
☐ I know the melodies of many songs or musical pieces.
☐ If is hear musical piece once or twice, I can easily repeat it.
☐ I often tap, whistle, hum or sing when engaged in a task.
☐ Total Musical boxes checked _____

INTERPERSONAL Section 6

☐ People often come to me to seek advice or counsel.
☐ I prefer team and group sports to individual sports.

☐ I have at least three close friends.
☐ I enjoy social pastimes like board games and charades more than individual ones such as video games and solitaire.

☐ I like the challenge of teaching other people what I know how to do.
☐ I have been called a leader and consider myself one.
☐ I am comfortable in a crowd of people.
☐ I am involved in local school, neighborhood, church and community activities.
☐ I would rather spend a Saturday night at a party than spend it at home alone.
☐ Total interpersonal boxes checked _____

INTRAPERSONAL Section 7

☐ I regularly spend time reflecting, meditating or thinking about important life questions.
☐ I have attended classes, seminars and workshops to gain insight about myself and experience personal growth.
☐ My opinions and views distinguish me from others.
☐ I have a hobby, pastime or special activity that I do alone.
☐ I have specific goals in life that I think about regularly.
☐ I have a realistic view of my own strengths and weaknesses backed up by accurate feeback from others.
☐ I would rather spend a weekend in a cabin or hide-away than at a large resort with lots of people.
☐ I am independent minded and strong willed.
☐ I keep a journal or diary to record the events of my inner life.
☐ I am self-employed or have seriously considered starting my own business.
☐ Total Intrapersonal boxes checked. _____

NATURALIST Section 8

☐ I categorized things by common traits.
☐ Ecological issues are important to me.
☐ Classification helps me make sense of new data.
☐ I enjoy working in a garden.
☐ Putting items in hierarchies makes sense to me.
☐ My home has a recycling system in place.
☐ I enjoy being in the outdoors, going camping, hiking, and working with animals.
☐ I enjoy studying biology, botany and or zoology.
☐ I pick up on suble differences in meaning.
☐ I believe in earth preservation, and global warming.
☐ Total number of Naturalist traits _____

METAPHYSICAL OR EXISTENIALIST Section 9

☐ I enjoy cosmological information and films.
☐ I enjoy science fiction subjects
☐ I enjoy meditation, conscious studies, or self development seminars
☐ I enjoy experiencing philosopher's concepts.
☐ Comparative religions interest me.
☐ I am interested in alternative healing techniques.

- ☐ Experimental psychological and paranormal events interest me.
- ☐ I enjoy discussion issues about the meaning of life, and realities.
- ☐ I enjoy learning about intelligent life in the universe.
- ☐ I like physics, astrology, astrometry, and metaphysical ideas.
- ☐ Total Number of Metaphysical traits _____

SURVEY TESTS DATA

Age_____

Ethnicity_____

Birth place_____

Went to school_____(graduation)

Location_____

College graduation_____(yes or no)

Foreign Language_____(yes or no)

Which one?_____

Culture_____

Sections	Total Forward	Multiply	Score
1		X10	
2		X10	
3		X10	
4		X10	
5		X10	
6		X10	
7		X10	
8		X10	
9		X10	

	Sec 1	Sec 2	Sec 3	Sec.4	Sec 5	Sec 6	Sec 7	Sec 8	Sec.9
100									
90									
80									
70									
60									
50									
40									
30									
20									
10									
0									

Plot your scores on the bar graph.

Notes

Dominant intelligence in Order.

REFERENCES

Ackerman, S. (1992). *Discovering the Brain*, Washington D.C.: National Academy Press.

Armstrong, T. (1994). *Multiple Intelligences in the Classroom,* Alexandria, VA: Association for Supervision and Curriculum Development.

Banks, J.A. (2003) *Cultural Diversity and Education, Foundations, Curriculum, and Teaching 5th edition.* Boston, MA: Pearson, Education, Inc.

Brackin, S.L. (2000). *Technology and the Visual Acquisition of Knowledge for the Multiple Intelligence Theory's.* Dallas, Texas: Visual Learner.

Baum, S. (1984) *Meeting the needs of learning disabled gifted students.* Roeper Review, 7(1), 16-19

Bogen, J. (1969) The other side of the brain: II. An oppositional mind. *Bulletin of the Los Angeles Neurological Society*, 34, 135-162.

Caine, G., Nummela-Caine, R., & Crowell, S. (1999) *Mindshifts: A Brain-Based Process For Restructuring Schools and Renewing Education, 2nd ed*AZ: Zephyr Press.

Caine, G., Nummela-Caine, (1997) *Education on the Edge of possibility*, Alexandria, VA: ASCD Association for Supervision and Curriculum Development.

Caine, R.N., & Caine, G. (1994). *Making Connections: Teaching and the Human Brain* New York: Addison-Wesley, Innovative Learning Publications.

Calhoun, E. Joyce, B., Well, M (2009) *Models of teaching and Learning*. Boston MA: Pearson Education Inc.

Campbell, L., Cambell, B., & Dickinson, D. (1993). *Teaching and learning through multiple Intelligences*. Tucson: Zephyr Press.

New Hampshire: Rivier College Press.

Das, J.P., Kriby, J.R, & Jarman, R,F, (1979). *Simultaneous and successive cognitive processes.* New York: Academic Press.

D'Arcangelo, M. (2000). How does the brain develop? A conversation with Steven Peterson *Educational Leadership*, 58(3), 68-71.

Diamond, M. & Hopson, J. (1999*) Magic Trees of the Mind: How to Nurture Your Child's Intelligences, Creativity, and Healthy Emotions from Birth through Adolescenc*e. New York: Plume.

Dixon, J.P. (1983). *The spatial child,* Springfield, IL: Charles C. Thomas.

Gardner, H. (1993*). Frames of mind, The theory of multiple intelligences.* New York: Basic Books.

Gardner, H. (1999*). Intelligence reframed.* New York: Basic Books.

Gardner, H. (1974). *The Shattered Mind,* New York, Random House.

Garritson, J. S. (1979). *Integrating Curriculum Through the Arts,* magazine: Child Arts.

Gaxiola, R. (2008). *Southern California Teacher's Perceptions on The Impact of Classroom Technology Use.* San Bernardino, CA: National University.

Hallahan, D.P.& Kauffman, J.M. (2000). *Exceptional Learners,* Needham Heights, publishers, Allyn Bacon.

Hanna, J. (2005*). Mind, Brain, & Education, Linking Biology, Neuroscience, & Educational Practice.* Boston MA: HGSE News, the news source of the Harvard Graduate School of Education.

Herrmann, N. (1995*). The Creative brain: Insights into creativity, communication, management, education, and self-understanding.* The Ned Hermann Group.

Hoerr, T.R. (2000) *Technology and MI.* New City School, St. Lous, MO: ASCD Press.

Jensen, E. (1998) *Teaching with the Brain in Mind.* Alexandria, VA: ASCD Association for Supervision and Curriculm Development.

Katzir, T. & J. Pare-Blagoev, (2003) "Applying cognitive neuroscience research to education. The case of Literacy". *Educational Psychologist*, (41(1): p. 53-74.

Kirk S. A., (1993*) Educating Exceptional Children, journal,(7)* Boston, Houghton Mifflin.

Lazear, D. (1991). *Seven ways of knowing: Teaching for multiple intelligences.* Palatine, Skylight.

Lehmkyhl, D. & Lamping, D.C. (1993*) Organizing for the Creative Person.,* New York, Three Rivers Press.

Levy-Argresti, J., & Sperry, R. (1968). Differential perceptual capacities in major and Minor Hemispheres. *Proceedings of the National Academy of Sciences,* 61.1151.

Lumsdaine, E., Lumsdaine, M.& Shelnutt, J.W. (1999*). Creative Problem Solving and Engineering Design.* McGraw-Hill, Inc.

Luria, A.R. (1966). *Higher cortical functions in man.* New York: Basic Books.

Maker, C.J. (1982). *Curriculum development for the gifted*, Rockville, MD: Aspen, CO.

Maker, C.J. & Nielson, A.B. (1995), *Teaching Models in Education of the Gifted*, (2) Austin, Pro-Ed.

Ornstein, A.C., Levine, D.U. (2008). *Foundations of Education 10*[th] *ed.* Boston MA: Houghton Mifflin Company.

Shearer, B.C. (2006) *Using a Multiple Intelligences Assessment to Facilitate Teacher* Development. Kent Ohio: MI Research, and Consulting, Inc.

Silverman, L.K., Chitwood, D.G., & Waters, J.L. (1986). Young gifted children: *Topics in Early Childhood Special Education, 6(1), 23-24*.

Silverman, L.K. (1986). *Characteristics of Introversion in Children.* Denver, CO, Gifted Child Development Center.

Ward, M.E., (2003) *The Balance Curriculum, Educating the Whole Child.* Ralaigh, NC: NC Department of Public Instruction.

Wetzel, D.R. (2009). *7 Technology Tips for the classroom.* (http://teaching technology.suite101. com/Article.cfm/7_technology_to[s_fpr-the_classroom).

Zull, J.E. (2002). *The Art of Changing the Brain: Enriching the Practice of teaching by Exploring the Biology of Learning.* Sterling VA: Stylus Publishing.

CURRICULUM VITAE

Joyce Diane Schulz graduation from Millikan High School, Long Beach, California, in 1958. She received her Bachelor of Arts from California State University at Los Angeles 1967. Her State teaching credentials in 1977 in Single Subject in Art. Her second teaching credential in 1981 a multiple subjects credential K-12, adult education. She has been teaching in California for over thirty years, and is now retired from the Public Schools. She has received her Master of Arts in Education from Argosy University in December 2010.

Joyce Diane Schulz

Director of the Whole Mind Center of Education.
*Tutoring
K-12 Adults
Consultant
*Creative Arts
*Percussion
*Meditation
*Astrologer
*Senior Mind-body balancing programs.

Joyce Diane Schulz MAed, BA has been a public school educator for over 30 years, and now a Consultant in Whole Brain Theory of Education for the struggling learner. She has developed a system of learning which supports all ages and subjects that makes learning fun. It does not matter how old or young you are, her program can help you find greater joy in learning and life. Contact Joyceds@Live.com

authorHOUSE®

ISBN 978-1-4567-6071-7
90000
9 781456 760717